Underground Rock Stars

Patricia Pike

DEDICATION
To my family.

Underground Rock Stars

Whetu and his Grandfather were sitting around a campfire enjoying the smell of cooking eel and trying to ignore their stomachs growling as they wait for their dinner.

"Koro." Whetu said, "Tell me the story about the stars and the glowworms, please."

His Grandfather looked into the skies above them and took a deep breath as he started the tale.

"Do you see the glow worms Moko? The ones amongst the trees and in the mouths of the tomo? Well, I will tell you how it all began. It was before man walked on this land. A time when the sky and the land were one great mass. There was great love between the earth and the sky, in fact the children felt there was no place for them in their parent's lives. Their children grew tired of this. Tumatauenga even wanted to kill them both. Rongo the god of food tried to push them apart. Tangaroa, the god of the sea tried, but he too was not strong enough. Haumia-tiketike, god of wild food joined him, but still the parents were locked together.

"Tane Mahuta, God of forests and wild birds pushed and pushed until the land and the sky separated with a roar of pain and grief. Ranginui and Papatuanuku were devastated. Ranginui rained tears down from the sky to show her love. Papatuanuku sent up mists into the heavens. Except the children of the Earth and Sky were happy. Only Tawhirimatea grumbled his complaint and joined his father in anger against his brothers. He whipped up winds and storms, great tempests raged across the land. Soon the cultivated and wild food were left in tatters. Tane Mahuta watched as his great trees and birds were tossed to and fro."

"Koro is that why it is not good to stand under a tree when the lightning strikes?"

"Moko you are clever and have learned well. But I have not told you how the stars came to be yet. Let us carry on."

"Tawhirimatea, the God of the weather, was so angry that his parents were separated, that he ripped out his eyes and threw them into the skies, where they formed the stars. Stars which would stay constant and true and be a guide for travellers throughout the ages. The stars themselves were soon shining down from the heavens. There was Waipuna-a-rangi, and Uru-a-rangi, Waita and of course Matariki or the eyes of the God.

"Tawhirimatea raged over the earth and with lightning and thunder, winds and waves he showed his displeasure. He shook Tane Mahuta's trees until their leaves lay strewn on the ground. But for all his anger the earth found its rhythm and seasons came and went. And life was good and plants grew.

"Rivers lazily wound their way through great mountains and fields of green. Animals inhabited the land and the birds sang in the trees and insects scuttled through the undergrowth. Man had not yet set his feet upon the land of Papatuanuku and the Gods were free to roam the countryside. The trees in Tane Mahuta's kingdom stretched their roots deep into the earth and their leaves tangled amongst the clouds. Tawhirimatea still raged on at times and there were gentle days with soft breezes as well as the tumult and storms."

"Koro, I love the feel of rain on my face. I also like it when the sun shines. I think I love all the seasons." Whetu said and smiled quietly to himself. His favourite was the Autumn with its trees that looked like they were on fire.

Koro continued on with his tale.

"In the caves of Waitomo all remained dark. No illumination shone on the dripping stalactites or stalagmites as they formed one drop at a time. Their beauty remained hidden far from the light. The rain which fed the forests, trickled down through the earth and slowly carved out caves. Rivers ran through the gloom, in and out of caverns so stunningly spectacular that even the Gods themselves were in awe of the creation. The waters looked up and sighed as they slid beneath a cathedral of divine beauty. Colours and shapes graced the caverns like architectural marvels and, if you listened carefully, you might hear choirs of angels singing their joy. Can you hear them now, Whetu?"

"No, Koro, what do they sound like?"

"It's in the voice of the Ruru or the click of a gecko my child. Close your eyes and listen."

"I think I hear them now, Koro."

"Near Ranginui, Ra, the Sun shone during the daytime and at night, Marama the Moon reigned supreme. The stars disliked Marama, a big blob of rock just hanging in the sky. She never spoke to the distant twinkles and they grew angry with her. The stars whispered amongst themselves, plotting to destroy Marama and her arrogance. It was during Matariki, the time of remembering the dead and celebrating new life, that things came to a head. Plucking rocks from the ether, they threw asteroids at the Moon and dented her surface. The more they threw, the more the Moon laughed. Her smile seemed to grow with each rock that was thrown. This continued for time immemorial until the stars sighed in defeat and put down their arsenal. The Moon stayed strong, if a little bit dented. Marama shrugged off the scars and lifted her chin with dignity."

Grandfather looked up at the moon and Whetu tried to see where the rocks had dented its surface.

"Are those marks from the asteroids? Wow, those stars sure must have been angry." Whetu chuckled with delight as the moon shone brightly above him.

"It was then that the Caves of Waitomo added their voice to the story.

'Dear sisters of the skies, lend me your ears and hear. For I have a solution that will help us both.'

At first the stars did not listen. What could a lowly cave in a tiny corner of an island do to help them, the great and glorious stars of heaven? They plotted and they planned, but nothing they did seemed right for their situation. Matariki and Uru-a-rangi grunted in disgust.

'What can you do in your tiny country and on your small piece of earth? Surely you do not think you are greater than us?'

Finally Tupu-a-nuku and Waiti, the gentle stars, turned their view down to the earth. The corner of the world now known as Aotearoa. Yes, Whetu, right here in our little patch of the universe. Maybe right under your feet. And the stars right above us. Can you see the Pleiades constellation of stars? No, you are right. It only shows itself in the chill of Winter, but now on a warm Summer night, it is hidden behind the Earth. But it was those very stars that were instrumental in what happened next.

"'Tane Mahuta!' They called for they knew that he would be able to guide them with his wisdom. Tane Mahuta moved close to the caves and in a voice of great power said to the stars above.

'Listen! For not all good ideas come from the strong. Was it not I who saved this great land? And now I stand and listen to the birds of the forest, the Weta and Eel. They each have their story to tell.'

Looking up through his great leaves, he smiled and added. 'How has it helped your cause all these long years to throw your missiles at the Moon? Has it swayed her one iota? Maybe the caves have the answer if you would just pay heed.'

"Whetu can you guess what the plan could be?"

"No, Koro, he must be very wise to know how to solve that problem because I haven't got a clue."

"Tane Mahuta bowed his head and swayed in the breeze. Matariki and Uru-a-rangi glanced at each other across the great expanse of the sky. They nodded and waited to see what the caves could say for themselves. Tupu-a-nuku and Waiti gathered the lesser stars and told them to shush their bickering because something of great worth was about to come to pass. Even the planets turned to hear what was to be decided. The moon seemed to be sleeping, but she too was listening carefully. For this might be a concern to him. She was sure of her powers, because she knew that she could shift the waters of the world to her will and surely Waitomo was not of any great threat to Marama the Moon?

"Did you know that the Moon could move the sea, Whetu? We call it the tides and it's important to know them if you are ever to become a good fisherman, my boy.

"Waitomo started with a sigh, 'Well, we understand your feelings of playing second fiddle to the radiance of the Moon when your beauty is so great and glorious. We too have beauty that is hidden from sight. What we propose is that you use energy to make baby stars instead of throwing stones at the Moon.' And they stopped for effect. 'The Heavens are harsh for little ones we know. So send them to us to nurture and grow. Their light will shine on our wondrous creations, so others can marvel at us too. When the stars are bigger and stronger, we will send them back to you to form new star formations. You who lead sailors to safety, you who shine when the Moon is asleep, you are beautiful and soon the world will see that you are prettier by far than that old pockmarked Moon.'

That seemed like a cunning and clever way to solve a dispute. A lot of compliments and a little bit of advice. It's a good plan to follow in life. If you ever get into an argument with others, remember the lesson the caves have taught. Listen carefully to the problem, let them say their piece and then tell them of all their good qualities. They will be more open to your advice."

Koro chuckled. He had not always heeded this sage advice and when he was young there were many times of anger in his life. Now he was older and was trying to pass on his wisdom so that his grandson might avoid the pitfalls of life.

"Matariki called a meeting of all the stars both near and far. Numberless stars met for the decision. Some were for it and others against. A vote was taken and Tane Mahuta took his time counting them all.

'Three billion against.' He intoned with much gravity. 'Sixty five billion and forty five million, two thousand, three hundred and two have voted for the action.'

The Heavens shook with such glee. The Caves hummed with joy and now things became interesting. How were they supposed to make this work? Tawhirimatea sent a gentle breeze through the caves to show his pleasure. He was happy that his eyes were once again involved in the decisions of Aotearoa, the land of the long white cloud. All the brothers united as they came together in unity. Tangaroa sent his water up through the rivers so that he too could take part. Even Ranginui and Papatuanuku listened, but they didn't say a word as their sons went through different ideas. Some were not feasible and some were too silly to be taken seriously.

Matariki and the brothers scratched their heads and planned. The answer was simply brilliant. Each baby star would start out as a glow worm! Insect to egg, egg to worm, worm to pupa and round and round it would go. The longest time in their lives was when they glowed in the darkness and it was then that the best, biggest, greatest glow worm was chosen. This glow worm would be placed on the back of a little bat and out of the cave it would fly. Up, up, up into the night sky. The little bat would search for the furthest star. Rangi would sprinkle gentle dew on the little insect and it would be kept safe from harm in the haven of the bat's fur. Whetu, have you seen any bats tonight?"

"Yes Koro, just as the sun was setting. They came out of the caves and flew into the sky."

"Well, the little glowworm cannot live without moisture around it, so keeping it safe in a bat's fur was a clever decision."

"As the bat reached the limits of its flight, a splash of star dust settled around them both and surrounded them with magic. Matariki shone down on the pair and Waiti would send lesser stars to guide them on their way. Even the Southern Cross would unfold her arms and offer her protection. Waipuna-a-rangi blew soft winds to help them on their way and they finally reached their destination. A nursery, a school, a place of safety and filled with love and kindness."

Koro pointed up into the Milky Way where multitudes of stars shone down on them.

"Gee, Koro, there are lots of places for a small star to grow. Those stars look so small I don't think I could count them all even if I sat here all year."

"No, Whetu, maybe not. Do you know what your name means? Whetu means star." And Koro smiled as he ruffled his grandson's hair.

"The bat would be crowned with glory and waited on by asteroids for time immemorial. The glow worm would be taught the secrets of the universe. She would be taught day by day, precept by precept. There were times for fun too. She would search out her special bat friend and they would frolic and tumble through the skies. They danced around the Milky Way, rode the tails of comets and crept up close to tickle the Moon. One day the time came when the glow worm would graduate and make her way to the skies above Aotearoa. She would look down at her home and wait for the next glow worm to start its journey. Excited at the prospect of a new friend in the skies."

"I have friends Koro. Some at school, some at home and some at church and on the Marae. We have lots of fun."

"Each year at the time of Matariki, when Aotearoa shivers in the chill of Winter. The dead are remembered and people hope for the start of Spring; kites are flown in the skies. Each one trying hard to reach the stars. Each fragile creation fluttering and turning in the winds far above the Earth, trying, striving to emulate the flight of the bat and its precious cargo. Humans stand with their hands on the strings, tugging and encouraging their pieces of paper and wood to stay afloat until the stars reach down and pluck them from the skies. Tawhirimatea adds his breath to the endeavours of man and Tane Mahuta playfully tangles the kites in his branches. And for a moment the fight between the Godly brothers is laid to rest, and then the night falls and the stars reign supreme and humans go home to bed. Let us eat our eel, my boy. I think the gods of the land and sea have blessed us tonight. We have food enough for even the gods to enjoy."

Whetu and his grandfather ate the kumara, the eel and the water cress on big slabs of rewena bread. For pudding they ate huhu grubs dipped in honey and went to bed amongst the ferns with their pukus full, happy with their day.

Just as they slipped into sleep Koro saw a new star blinking in the sky above him. A family of bats were hunting for insects and the call of the more-pork added a lullaby to the night. Koro dreamed of the Atua of the land, sea and sky in harmony and man living happily. In Waitomo, a new star is formed. A new light starts to twinkle, a new bat is prepared to act as guardian. And each night humans look into the heavens and search out the birthplace of the smallest of stars. The place where it all began. Waitomo feels the kiss of the water as it caresses the sides of the caves, they feels the sway of the glow worms and they smile in satisfaction. All is well with the world. Whetu hears the celestial choirs singing around him and snuggles down into the ferns with a smile on his face. Man and nature at peace with each other.

<u>About the Author</u>

Patricia Pike a former South African now living in rural New Zealand. She lives with her husband and her two cats. Her grown children live all around the world and also close by. Family is very important to her.

She has been interested in art all her life. Story telling has just evolved over time.

Living near the Waitomo caves has given her an interest in the local legends and stories.

THANK YOU.